KARL MARX

by MURRAY WOLFSON

 Columbia University Press

NEW YORK AND LONDON   1971

COLUMBIA ESSAYS ON THE GREAT ECONOMISTS
DONALD J. DEWEY, GENERAL EDITOR

Karl Marx is Number 3 of the series

Copyright © 1971 Columbia University Press
ISBN: 0–231–03146–7
Library of Congress Catalog Card Number: 79–147310
Printed in the United States of America

ACKNOWLEDGMENTS: I have been greatly aided over many years by the friendship, encouragement, and gentle skepticism of Professor Martin Bronfenbrenner. It was he, as well as Professor Peter Wiles, who suggested that Marx might be studied through the "transformation problem." I am grateful to them, and to my colleagues at Oregon State University, Professors R. C. Vars, Richard Towey, Harry Goheen, and David Carlson for much patient help and earnest discussion. None of them are responsible for my errors or opinions. This booklet was produced through the kind encouragement of Professor Donald Dewey, and by Bernard Gronert of Columbia University Press. My wife Betty helped most of all.

PREFACE

Some years ago, under the influence of positivist philosophy, it used to be the fashion to consider statements in a three-fold classification: True, False, Meaningless. This trichotomy is still useful in the positive science to which it refers. If our arguments have empirical meaning, they can be tested by experimental or other factual evidence; if tests are impossible, then we are making statements that can have no consequences since the possibility of factual inferences from our statements provides an opportunity for test.

Subsequent reflection convinced many that "meaningless" and "nonsense" do not mean the same thing. A collection of symbols BJY&! % 'KB?D" # is not only meaningless but nonsense. So are self-contradictory statements like: "It will rain today and it will not rain today." These may be safely ignored since the words and symbols communicate nothing. But what of this passage from *The Art of the Fugue?*

These symbols have several meanings, yet none of them are factual: They are imperatives to produce a set of as yet unheard sounds. They have an anagrammatic meaning, BACH, in

German musical usage where B-flat is written as B, and B is written H. They have musical meaning of an esthetic and nonverbal sort.

Combined in Marx's economic writings are meanings of both scientific and ethical import which we will try to sort out. The task is difficult because Marx viewed himself as a scientist and his normative expressions are wrapped up in his objective science, yet I feel that they have to be evaluated separately. I think that the current tendency to view Marx as "really" a moralist overstates the case, since the nub of Marxism is that these two meanings are not separable. The truth of the matter is that important elements of his science are wrong, but his identification of social welfare with the condition of the proletarians continues to attract many as a valid social ethic.

CLASS, LABOR, AND HISTORY

THE COMMUNIST MANIFESTO asserts: "The history of all hitherto existing society is the history of class struggles." All else that Marx wrote is really commentary on this thesis.

John Stuart Mill contended just the opposite. In *A System of Logic*, he argued that social analysis, like natural science, must ultimately be an inductive inference from the immediate atomic facts of experience. In economics, these facts were taken to be behavior of individual human beings. Successive generations of neoclassical theorists were to infer utility functions underlying the preferences revealed by individuals in market choices. Once given the preference patterns of individuals, it was possible, in light of the "state of technical arts" to account for the allocation of resources, distribution of income, and the values of commodities.

Few philosophers of science would quarrel with the aims of Mill's empirical method. Knowledge is acquired from experience, and since we cannot experience a generalization, scientific knowledge must be an inference from particular facts about the uniformities we must presume to exist in nature. But surely it is improper to justify statements about the causes of events by an appeal to empiricism. Study of particular facts is not equivalent to an assertion that the world is *made up of* particular things, objects, or people. The difficulties of this position are famous: What are the relations between things? How might general qualities such as round or hot inhere in a thing?

We make the atomic statements about the facts of our experience. What we consider facts depends on our theories about how experience is expected to fit together. Fruitful theories are those which are consistent statements, not falsified by the facts to which they refer, which predict results in which we are interested. Doubtless many problems are solved by Mill's thesis that the history of hitherto known societies is the history of the individuals who compose them. Nevertheless in other contexts society might be regarded as the facts of the evolution of primates, of aggregations of protein molecules, or, as Marx suggested, the interaction of classes.

When economists grapple with practical problems of group interests, Marx's analysis often reappears in new terminology. Despite Keynes's insistence that he could make no "sense out of K.M." the aggregation of national product into consumption and investment goods and the consequent identity of savings and investment is very closely related to the "reproduction schema" to be found in the second volume of *Capital*. Subsequent discussion by Keynes's followers at Cambridge has pushed closer to Marx.

Keynes's partition of national income into consumption and investment describes the commodities purchased rather than the division of income between workers and capitalists. However Nicholas Kaldor has shown how the Keynesian system implies a class distribution of income:

> Income [Y] may be divided into two broad categories, Wages and Profits (W and P), where the wage-category comprises not only manual labor, but salaries as well, and Profits the income of property owners generally, and not only of entrepreneurs; the important difference between them being in the marginal propensities to consume (or save), wage earners' marginal savings being small in relation to those of capitalists.

Writing S_w and S_p, for aggregate savings out of Wages and Profits, we have the following income identities:

$$Y = W + P$$
$$I = S$$
$$S = S_w + S_p.$$

Taking investment as given, and assuming simple proportional savings functions $S_w = s_w W$ and $S_p = s_p P$, we obtain.

$$I = s_p P + s_w W = s_p P + s_w(Y - P) = (s_p - s_w)P + s_w Y.$$

Whence
$$\frac{I}{Y} = (s_p - s_w)\frac{P}{Y} + s_w$$

and
$$\frac{P}{Y} = \frac{1}{s_p - s_w}\frac{I}{Y} - \frac{s_w}{s_p - s_w}.$$

Thus, given the wage-earners' and the capitalists' propensities to save, the share of profits in income depends simply on the ratio of investment to output. [pp. 228–29]

In Mill's footsteps, the Cambridge economists treat the decision of capitalists to invest—their "animal spirits"—as the independent variable. Together with the propensities of individuals to save and consume, it is the determinant of class income. Yet Kaldor's identities only show that capital accumulation must be consistent with the distribution of income, Marx took as his basic datum the _conflict of classes_ which determined distribution. Given the state of the class struggle, the ratio of investment to income is determined.

Marx expressed the division of income into shares by the rate of surplus value. We designate this ratio by σ. It represents the income of the whole capitalist class (profits, rents, and interest) divided by that of the workers, measured in hours of homogeneous labor. Marx believed that all new value added arose solely from the efforts of labor. Value alloted to workers, he called _variable_ capital because during the process of production it was self-expanding to yield *surplus value* to the capitalists. The rate of surplus value is then:

$$\sigma = \frac{\text{surplus value}}{\text{variable capital}} = \frac{s}{v}.$$

The rate of surplus value differs from Kaldor's P/Y in an accounting sense. Marx compares labor time, while Kaldor and Keynes deal in money income. Marx's surplus value is measured at the point when commodities have been sold and payment made for labor (variable capital) and for means of production (constant capital) used up. The surplus value may then be consumed by the capitalists, or accumulated as *additional* variable capital or constant capital. Keynes measures the division of income after surplus value has been allocated. The portion of surplus value which is reinvested in an enlarged labor force by a firm counts as wages. This is made clear if, wih Kaldor, we neglect workers' savings by setting $s_w = 0$; and treat the capitalists as pure accumulators by ignoring their consumption, setting $s_p = 1$. Then from the Kaldor equations, profit is equal to investment in constant capital, $P = I$.

Analysis of economic aggregates common to Marx and Keynes is more important than their differences. The fact of aggregation requires a common unit of measure, labor or money value. Macroeconomics must discuss *value* flows as shares of income divided between capitalists and workers, or consumption and investment.

The Kaldor identities hold regardless of whether national income is at the full employment level or not, since only the *proportions* of investment and profits to income are determined. Hence if investment and income increase in the same proportion, then the relative shares of income going to workers and capitalists would be unaffected. Both could be increased toward full employment levels of income without requiring that the equilibrium of class incomes be disturbed. In the context of the Great Depression, Keynes was in effect suggesting that a class truce was possible up to a level of income approaching full employment, without, as had been suggested by the "classical economists," the burden of recovery being shifted to the workers. For the duration of the depression, the rate of surplus value could remain unchanged, to the joint advantage of workers and capitalists.

I think this was the message of "sticky" money wages. Couched in Millian terms as if myopic workers were possessed of "money illusion," it was in effect a proposal for public policy which would respect class lines. This can be clearly seen if it is combined with Keynes's approximation that employment is proportional to money income as long as there is a large amount of unemployment.

Let $\quad \bar{w}$ = money wages (taken as constant)

$\qquad n$ = employment

$\qquad Y$ = money national income,

then $\quad n = kY$

and $\quad \bar{w}n = \bar{w}kY$

hence $\dfrac{\bar{w}n}{Y} = \bar{w}k$.

Since the right hand side is constant, so if the left, which represents labor's share in income.

By expressing class attitudes and interests in terms of the individual behavior patterns of its constituent individuals, Keynes set the stage for an investigation of the conditions for class compromise. The human propensities to save and consume and the money illusion of workers are taken as outside the operational domain of public policy. Keynes investigated the conditions for making full employment and growth consistent with them. Keynes's great achievement was to demonstrate the existence of mutually useful compromises which fundamentally retain the class shares of income. If microeconomic equilibrium represents the equilibrium of individual desires, macroeconomic equilibrium represents the balancing of the groups in society.

Marx was interested in revolution, not compromise. He focused on conditions in which propensities, illusions, and animal spirits were variable. He strove to show that class consciousness was propelled by objective forces which ultimately made compromise impossible. In the long run, individual attitudes were significant only insofar as they reflected the changing group interests, and the exploitation of labor made classes inherently antagonistic.

Marx's analysis is based on the labor theory of value and is either tautologous or unsatisfactory. Purporting to be a positive statement that the exchange values of commodities are equal to the "average socially necessary labor time required to reproduce them," the labor theory of value is offered as an explanation of long-run equilibrium price. Labor-power, the workers' capacity for labor, sells at its historically determined subsistence cost of human reproduction. Since the value of labor-power is less than the labor actually expended by the worker, unearned surplus value accrues to the capitalist. Labor is exploited by capital.

An empirical explanation of class behavior in terms of contingent historically evolved social *attitudes* was unacceptable to Marx because it cannot forecast future class consciousness. History would not be determinate. In a mature statement, the preface to *A Critique of Political Economy*, ideology was said to be derivative of the circumstances of production. Marx made use of the philosophical radicals who argued that individuals were the creature of their conditioning. Ranks of reformers, such as James Mill and his Victorian son, strove to manipulate the environment to uplift the common man by education and improving his condition of life. Yet, "The educator," Marx retorted "must himself be educated." His education—ideals, ethics, morals, institutions—are the product of class society and must therefore necessarily reflect the ideology of the ruling class, at least during the period of its ascendency. For his science of society Marx needed a theory of social classes based on an independent driving force of history which he found in the evolution of production. The "superstructure" of ideology and its legal and institutional implementation was derivative of the development of production.

Marx's dichotomous definition of classes is legal as well as materialistic: they are distinguished by whether their members own or do not own the means of production. The essence of class development is entailed in its definition, in Marx. Each historical stage of production requires a unique class structure since each technology requires a distinctive organization of the labor force and productive property. Institutions must be congruent with the fundamental class relations as the "mode of production." The evolutionary social process is seen by Marx as uniquely determined by the unidirectional material progress in the mode of production which takes place independently of human will or consciousness.

Stated baldly, a philosophy of history which deals in historical essences is so clearly wrong that many contemporary scholars have occupied themselves with attributing it to Engels rather than Marx. (Kamenka; Lichtheim; Williams). Yet the difficulties are inherent in Marx's doctrine. If the stages of society are to succeed one another in a predetermined way, they must be driven by an entity that does *not* change. Hence

Marx must require the evolution of the impersonal "forces of production" leading from one "mode" to another to be self-caused. The drive to technical progress must be permanent and impersonal. In general, human will in class or individual form may only be considered irrelevant to succeeding conditions, if there exists only a single outcome of economic growth determined by objective conditions. But there are many growth paths. Since the accumulation of capital implies a decision to delay present satisfactions in favor of future incomes, it is unavoidable that these actions help determine the "forces of production." Precisely the Puritan ideology of such future-oriented persons as Adam Smith and Joseph Stalin made for high rates of savings and capital accumulation. Marx himself pointed out an underdeveloped country counter-example in static "Asiatic society" where production does not advance.

"Superstructure" is of decisive importance to growth through technical change. It is true that in most historical circumstances, scientific knowledge expands. But the direction it takes, the factors of production it seeks to economize in its technical application, the approbation accorded new knowledge, the acceptance of social change it entails, all depend on attitude and ideology. Labor surplus in classical Rome and contemporary underdeveloped nations resulted in economic decay; in eighteenth-century England it meant explosive growth.

If the view attributed to Engels is too crude, what are the alternatives? Marxism may be hedged into meaninglessness, by viewing every failure of the doctrine as a temporary influence of ideology retarding the ultimate forward flux of production.

More plausibly, Marxism can be read as history. Looking backward, it is possible to show that institutional superstructure has from time to time come to be out of kilter with production. Qualitatively new forms of social organization—capitalism, feudalism, slavery—as well as new technologies sprang up as the result of the obsolescence and incongruence of the old. Beyond doubt, one might give a Marxist account of events *after the fact*. Quantitative changes in production may well bring on qualitative changes in social organization. However, it is not possible to predict the new quality in advance of the actual occurrences. Qualitative change implies a uniqueness of the outcome of antitheses in the prior stage of society which precludes the very uniformity needed for prediction. Marxism is useful for interpreting history, but it is not a scientific basis for changing it.

John Stuart Mill saw this weakness in the historical method in social science despite his fatuous Victorian belief in progress and the perfectability of man. (Bk. V, ch. x) His criticism has been expanded in most vigorous consistent form by Karl Popper (see References), who denies the possibility of prediction from qualitatively singular, unique, occurrences. Induction requires uniformity, since it proceeds from events which it claims are *alike*, not different. The generalization thus achieved forms the basis for *deductive* hypotheses about future events. But deduction from any premises cannot contain more information than was originally contained in them—in this case experience with the past.

Marx once remarked, "The philosophers have only *interpreted* the world in various ways; the point however is to *change* it." The world may very well need changing. But we cannot abdicate personal responsibility for change in favor of the autonomous working of the historical process. Since human will can affect events, there is no escaping a moral accounting for our value judgments about social goals and their costs. Furthermore, we must reckon with the tentative nature of our inductive conclusions. As Mill argued so forcefully, the uncertainty inherent in social science requires us to preserve dissent as a matter of practical necessity. Marx's pursuit of the will-o'-the-wisp of certainty led the youthful libertarian to a doctrine which ultimately hardened into dogmatism.

Marx's theory of history is neither an inductive generalization nor a deduction from singular historical events. Rather, it is an attempt to deduce information about society from the *essential nature of Man*. Over and over again, Marx and Engels assert that man is by nature a laboring creature.

Labor was the title Hegel assigned to the struggle of Mind to appropriate the concrete world of nature "into" Reason. For Marx, labor was practical human activity aimed at making nature the instrument of human purpose. Marx stood Hegel "on his head" and argued that the ultimate reality was not the Idea, but Matter. The history of mankind was essentially the conflict between active human beings, and the purposeless contingent external world. Through labor, man sought to make the material world something for himself. In the course of this cycle, both the material world and man undergo progressive change. Unlike consumption, which is individual, labor is a social act. Man expresses his social purpose through production.

Private ownership of the means of production has as its purpose the exclusion of non-owners from the income which, in a "fetishistic" manner, becomes imputed to the property. Yet production, Marx argued, is the expenditure of labor. The institution of private property makes it impossible for man to overcome the alienation and return his effort to himself. Class society shows itself to be irrational at each stage of development. The State is instituted by the ruling class to protect property by force and perpetuate labor alienation.

"Irrational" has two meanings for Marxism. It can be used to describe objective conflicts between the forces of production and institutional superstructure when a new order is nascent within the integument of the old. It is also a proposal that society *ought* to be changed. It is irrational for labor to be permanently alienated from the worker. Man ought not to be demeaned by the products of his own efforts. He ought not to be a mere commodity to be bought and sold on the market as a factor of production.

The young Marx, writing before 1845, took the second, humanistic, view. Society was "unphilosophical" and had to be set right by intellectual criticism of private property. At the hands of the German police authorities, Marx learned that value judgments are not subjects of rational discussion. Only in the dialectical fantasy of the ultimate returning of the alienated objectification of self into the subject, can one identify the idea that income *ought* to accrue to the workers, with the notion that it is *objectively* rational that the alienation of labor be-overcome.

When Marx attempted to do more than interpret the world, he had to find out how it worked. He needed a positive social science. From this point, Marx's work can be described as an attempt to subsume normative judgments into deterministic social science. Recent scholarship has stressed the continuity of his early views and the later science of society. It is foolish to underestimate the shift in emphasis. By the time Marx jotted down the *Theses on Feuerbach* (1845), later included in the *German Ideology* (1846), he was looking for the practical roots of alienation as an historical process. The *Communist Manifesto* (1848) is a complete reversal of Marx's earlier views. He and Engels excoriate "German Socialism" and its philosophical critique of alienation for failing to accept the deterministic theory of class struggle necessary for the practicing revolutionary.

13

The outcome is not the abandonment of humanism altogether, but its historical, materialistic, and class reinterpretation. It is not private property as such which makes Man less than a human being, but that *capitalism* uses private property to exploit the *workers*. (*Poverty of Philosophy*). In the critically important discussion of the "fetishism of commodities" in the first volume of *Capital* (1867) the mature Marx makes clear that he thinks of human labor in two ways: as the ultimate cost of production internal to the firm, it explains the facts of exchange; as the sole social cost, it permits a social welfare calculation from the point of view of the working class. Marx identified these two meanings with each other.

It is for this reason that Marx slaved to demonstrate the trend of capitalism toward self destruction from the labor theory of value. The immense labor of writing *Capital* as a scientific treatise in political economy is not otherwise explicable. The alienation of labor under capitalism was irrational, Marx finally concluded in *A Critique of Political Economy*, because the system was already shown to be doomed by the inevitable march of history. "Mankind always takes up only such problems as it can solve; since, looking at the matter more closely, we will always find that the problem itself arises only when the material conditions necessary for its solution already exist. . . . The productive forces developing in the womb of bourgeois society create the material conditions for the solution of that antagonism. This social formation constitutes, therefore, the closing chapter of the prehistoric stage of human society."

2. LABOR AND SOCIAL COST

It is absurd to say that man is essentially a laboring animal. With equal justice one might say that he is essentially a biped, or a vocal animal, or a moral being, or a rational consumer. In *A Reappraisal of Marxian Economics* I traced out the dependence of Marx's positive theory of exchange—the labor theory of value—on the philosophy of essences. Here, instead of starting from the determinism in Marxian economics obvious from the first words in Volume I of *Capital*, let us take up the track in Volume II, subtitled *The Circulation of Commodities*.

We will simply record the interindustry flows of labor. In this way we can turn first to the social cost concept of labor and then to the problem of market valuation. We do not have to consider labor as the human essence to keep track of it. In order to do so we must not quibble and take labor as homogeneous. We do so with the proviso that we shall want to renege on our generosity later by insisting that the homogeneity can only be accomplished by making labor a subjective disutility of effort rather than Marx's material human activity.

Marx's scheme of "expanded reproduction," which for convenience we show here with rows and columns transposed, displays the circulation of labor in a two-sector economy. Department I produces means of production and Department II produces consumer goods. We are able to serve up Marx *à la* Leontief in this Labor Transactions Matrix.

LABOR TRANSACTIONS MATRIX

	I	II	Final Demand		Totals
			consumption	accumulation	
I	c_1	c_2	0	$\Delta C_1 + \Delta C_2$	w_1
II	v_1	v_2	$\theta_1 s_1 + \theta_2 s_2$	$\Delta v_1 + \Delta v_2$	w_2
Surplus labor	s_1	s_2	$s_1 + s_2$		
Totals	w_1	w_2			$w_1 + w_2$

For the i-th industry, c_i is the amount of labor that is expended on reproducing the *used up* constant capital: means of production such as raw materials, semifinished goods, stocks of fuels, and fixed constant capital such as machinery and buildings. Thus, c_i is the flow of labor into final products indirectly through an intermediate product. On Marx's further assumption that labor today is equivalent to labor tomorrow, capital consumption cannot transmit more labor than was originally embodied in the stock. Hence the *stock* of congealed labor used in production is called constant capital. We designate the stock with an upper-case C_i, and the flow of labor replacing capital consumption by lower-case c_i.

Variable capital, v_i, is the amount of labor expended in the consumption goods used up by workers. Marx defined the period of production so that it just equals the time required to use the stock of v once. Flows and stocks of variable capital are therefore identical. Man has been able since primitive times to expend more labor than is currently required for the reproduction of the labor force. Hence in Marx's system variable capital is self-expanding. It produces surplus labor, s_i, which in class societies accrues to the owners of the means of production. In bourgeois society it is the income imputed to the capitalists which Marx called surplus *value* because of his identification of labor and exchange value.

Surplus labor may be accumulated either in the form of more constant capital (ΔC_i) or a larger allocation for the labor force (Δv_i). It might be consumed by capitalists and other unproductive groups. The portion of s_i consumed we designate by θ_i.

The matrix rows show how the total labor used by Department I is allocated toward the production of constant capital used up by itself and Department II. Department I contributes nothing toward consumption, but it does provide the accumulated constant capital, $\Delta C_1 + \Delta C_2$. Department II supplies the needs of workers currently employed in both departments. Surplus labor from Department II is shown in the Final Demand columns to supply the capitalists' consumption $\theta_1 s_1 + \theta_2 s_2$, and also provides for augmented expenditures on labor $\Delta v_1 + \Delta v_2$. Consistency requires that the total of final demand equals total *net* surplus labor input $s_1 + s_2$.

This formal accounting tautology is not dependent on a labor theory of exchange value, nor is it restricted to a capitalist society. Indeed, in *Capital*, Marx comments that a communist society of "freely associated men" would still have to allocate scarce labor and account for it along such lines as these. In the *Critique of the Gotha Program* he inveighs with characteristic vigor against socialists who imagined that the end of capitalism would eliminate the need for surplus labor. A socialist society would need to grow through the accumulation of capital. It would have to provide for the sustenance of its own unproductive workers—the political agitators, salesmen, priests, and professors.

Why does Marx denounce capitalism? It cannot be the existence or even the amount of surplus labor. Surplus labor could only be dispensed with in an ultimate communist society in which all desires were satiated, no population growth occurred, and all technical change was embodied in the replacement of old depreciated capital equipment. Riotous living of the capitalists is not really Marx's complaint. On the contrary, he wrote a panegyric on the parsimony of the bourgeoisie in the *Communist Manifesto*. Twenty years later in *Capital* Marx exclaimed "Accumulate, accumulate! That is Moses and the prophets!" Certainly a high rate of saving has been the characteristic slogan of Marxist planners once in power. More

17

plausibly, Marx was offering a critique of the social cost implicit in the way capitalism went about accumulation through the market mechanism.

We shall attempt to use the interindustry matrix of labor flows to construct a normative Marxian welfare economics which evaluates alternative social goals in terms of class interests and investigates how they may be accomplished at minimum social cost. Social cost is defined as total surplus labor.

The stumbling block to distinguishing normative from positive concepts of value in Marx is the notion that the labor congealed in commodities is actually equal to their exchange values under capitalism. We shall show that if this were actually the case, capitalism would minimize social cost. Marx identified his own views on what should constitute social cost, with a positive statement of the production costs internal to the capitalist firm. These are not the same. Under the capitalist rules of the game—for better or worse—the use of scarce property requires that its owner receive the same rate of profit as he gets by employing labor. Marx was fully aware that "values" had to be transformed into "prices of production" to account for the equalization of profit rates on industries with different capital-labor ratios. Instead of seizing upon the "transformation problem" as a means of criticizing capitalism, he regarded it as a secondary technical matter that had to be rationalized in such a way as not to threaten the labor theory of value.

The transactions matrix is converted into a technology matrix by dividing each of the elements of the interindustry quadrant by the corresponding column totals, w_j. Then $\gamma_i = c_i/w_j$ and $m_i = v_i/w_j$ describe the proportion of constant and variable capital embodied in each branch of production. Substituting $c_i = \gamma_i w_j$ and $v_i = m_i w_j$ into our transactions matrix, and lumping together the various final demands for each industry as F_1 and F_2:

$$\gamma_1 w_1 + \gamma_2 w_2 + F_1 = w_1$$
$$m_1 w_1 + m_2 w_2 + F_2 = w_2 \tag{1}$$

and hence:

$$(1 - \gamma_1)w_1 - \gamma_2 w_2 = F_1$$
$$-m_1 w_1 + (1 - m_2)w_2 = F_2. \tag{2}$$

Equation (2) can be solved for w_1 and w_2. (See Appendix Note 1.) Net social cost is the sum of the surplus labor in each department, $Z = s_1 + s_2$. Let π represent the ratio of surplus labor to total labor expended including both its congealed constant constituent and the variable and surplus elements. Then $\pi_j = s_j/w_j$ and the social cost function can be written:

$$Z = \pi_1 w_1 + \pi_2 w_2.$$

In a social system which permits free labor mobility, the rate of surplus labor, $\sigma_j = s_j/v_j$, will be made uniform by the migration of labor from one occupation to another seeking to maximize wage income and minimize work. (*Capital*, I, 206) It is also easy to see that since the proportion of variable capital to constant capital varies widely between industries, π, the surplus labor social cost divided by the total labor expended must also vary between industries. (See Appendix Note 2.) Given the final uses F_1 and F_2 each set of technical coefficients will require the expenditure of a certain amount of labor in each department, w_1 and w_2. These are shown in Figure 1 as B, B', B'', B'''.

Since labor resources may be used employing combinations of technologies, interpolations between the points B, B', B'', B''' are possible. These are drawn as linear in keeping with our input-output expository framework. While the combinations of points forming an open polygon convex to the origin are not the only ones feasible, they are the only efficient combinations. Points on the interior of the polygon would employ more labor for the same result than a point on the broken line. Furthermore, the interpolation *BB″* shown by the dotted line in Figure 1 would not be observed because it also would be interior. In the limit, if enough technologies could be identified

FIGURE 1

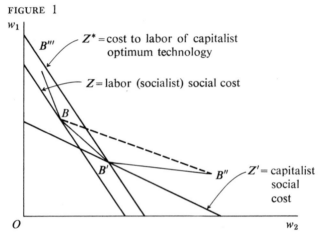

$B‴$ B $B′$ $B″$ would become a smooth curve. We call this an iso-accumulation line since it represents alternative inputs of gross labor which would result in equal satisfaction of final demand, F_1 and F_2.

Which of these technologies *ought* to be chosen? If we accept Marx's identification of social cost with uncompensated surplus labor, B is best. But if commodities are not valued in the capitalist market by their labor content, but by some other prices of production, then it is a different cost function which is minimized. If p_i represent the ratio of prices of production to values, such a cost function is $Z' = p_1\pi_1w_1 + p_2\pi_2w_2$. In Figure 1, the optimal point for capitalist market pricing is B'.

Marx showed that in general it is not the case that values and prices of production are identical ($p_i \neq 1$) and therefore the two cost functions to be minimized represent competing social criteria. Z is the labor or socialist, and Z' is the capitalist social cost function. On Marxian norms, the best of capitalist worlds, B', is unsatisfactory to labor because more surplus labor would be required to meet the accumulation goals. Graphically, the social cost *to labor* of choosing the technology best *for the capitalists* would be a line parallel to Z, but passing through B'. It is shown in Figure 1 as Z^*, and plainly lies beyond Z. (See Appendix Note 3.)

Prices of production, Marx argued, differ from values because in a capitalist society the rate of profit on the *total stock of capital* advanced by each firm must be equal. The rate of profit is $R = s/(C + v)$. The *capitalists* regard *all* of their outlay indifferently, whether it be constant or variable capital. They will migrate from one industry to another in response to profit incentives. At the same time the rate of surplus value must be equalized between occupations since *workers* compare the total labor they expend, $v + s$, with the *variable* capital payment to them. Marx showed that the rate of profit and the rate of surplus value are linked by the ratio of the stock of constant capital to the total stock of capital advanced, which Marx called the "organic composition of capital." If we designate the organic composition of capital for the i-th firm by q_i the rate of profit then becomes:

$$R_i = \frac{s_i}{C_i + v_i} = \left(\frac{s_i}{v_i}\right)\left(\frac{v_i}{C_i + v_i}\right) = \sigma\left(1 - \frac{C_i}{C_i + v_i}\right) = \sigma(1 - q_i).$$

Since q_i can be expected to differ for each industry, the other two ratios can only be equalized if prices of production differ from values. Firms with higher than average organic compositions would sell their goods above the labor value ($p > 1$); those with low organic composition would sell with prices of production below value ($p < 1$). (See Appendix Note 4.)

The obligatory equalization of the rate of returns to the *stock* of fixed capital is equivalent to saying each firm seeks the maximization of output subject to the constraint of a stock of resources. Hence, an imputed cost must be attached by the firm to all the elements of that stock. It follows that the higher prices of production of the industries with high organic composition are nothing but the interest cost imputed under capitalism to the large constant capital component which they employ. An unplanned capitalist economy with perfect competition between firms will autonomously move to that social optimum which treats interest and other property income as a social cost. Marx objected to this allocation, not because it was inefficient from the point of view of maximizing the physical product, but because it identified the internal, private costs of the capitalist firm with the cost to society.

Marx does not at all dispute that *capitalists* impute productivity to fixed capital. It is perfectly clear to him that the capitalist calculates interest on his stock whether or not he actually pays it over to a "money capitalist". (*Capital*, III, 443–44). Furthermore, the capitalist firm must deduct the opportunity cost of the more liquid alternative of an "interest bearing" use of capital when deciding to invest in "productive" enterprises. But he would insist that in social terms such property income is a transfer payment and not an addition of value. Only the myopia of the capitalist gives rise to the "preposterous" illusion that fixed capital is productive of value.

Marx's view of social cost is an ethical judgement. Yet, clearly the capitalist maximization of output subject to the

22

property constraint *also* entails an ethic: the notion that depriving an individual of control of his property for the period of production involves a psychic cost which ought to be overcome by persuasion rather than expropriation. As such, output maximization is not a purely rational calculation as a rational capitalist calculation. At the same time it is true that anyone charged with the responsibility of maximizing output with a limited supply of human and material resources will have to make this capitalist calculation. As has become increasingly clear, well-managed firms in the Soviet Union no less than capitalist enterprises must reckon an interest cost of capital as one of their internal costs. Interest, like land rent, or Alfred Marshall's quasi-rent on fixed capital, plays a critical role in the output-maximizing allocation of resources.

By what plan of action might the divergence between social and private costs be reconciled? There are two basic alternatives facing *every* society which accepts the existence of a dichotomy between individual and social viewpoints. We can identify them with points B and B' in Figure 1. B represents lower social cost to labor than B'. B' represents no less physical output than B, and probably more, depending on the inflexibility of technical substitution. Both B and B' satisfy the accumulation plan stated in value terms.

1. Planners might attempt to minimize social cost directly by choosing B. Having decided to accumulate a certain percentage of the national product— measured in money or labor terms—they would opt for the technology which minimizes social cost.

2. Planners might attempt to work for distributional equity indirectly by choosing B'. They might first choose the capitalist technology which maximizes physical output subject to the limitation of scarce labor and means of production. Only

then would they decide how much of the product they wish to accumulate. If there are technical limitations on production, B' must lie on a higher isoquant than B, since *all* resources are allocated in such a way as to maximize output. B is only a technical second best. Society would then attempt to compensate the workers by means of transfer payments which would make them at least as well off as at B. This is Lange-Lerner neo-classical socialism. Attempts to compensate labor by transfer payments while production is optimized on the capitalist principle are commonplace: they vary from the minimum wage laws and social security legislation to proposals more usually called "socialist."

The objections to this last procedure are well known. It is by no means evident that a consistent compensation principle can be found. The result of state-sponsored efficiency might be a more severe exploitation of the workers by the output maximizing planning elite than Marx attributed to private property. Further, the decentralization of profit incentive, if it is effective, conflicts with the compensation principle. It is difficult to imagine that the taxing away of profit is fully consistent with its use as an incentive. It is more likely that to one degree or another property-like vested interests would emerge which would have to be respected by the planners.

The first alternative is also open to objection. If output is restricted by a technically determined production function—even if that function is subject to technical progress at a limited rate—the increased output which becomes available at B' would permit a greater accumulation of capital and growth than at B. Hence, whether or not it is possible *now* to compensate workers for the extra surplus value, it might be more feasible to do so in the future. This possibility depends on both the increase in productivity, *and* on the subjective rate of discount with which workers now regard income to be received in years hence.

Multiplying w_1 and w_2 of each department in equation (2) by π_1 and π_2 and adding we get the total surplus labor in terms of final uses, F_1 and F_2.

$$S = \pi_1 w_1 + \pi_2 w_2 = T_1 F_1 + T_2 F_2$$

where

$$T_1 = \frac{\pi_1(1 - m_2) + \pi_2 m_1}{(1 - \gamma_1)(1 - m_2) - m_1 \gamma_2}$$

and

$$T_2 = \frac{\pi_1 \gamma_2 - \pi_2(1 - \gamma_1)}{(1 - \gamma_1)(1 - m_2) - m_1 \gamma_2}.$$

The slope of the frontier indicates the shadow price of accumulation in F_1 in terms of F_2 foregone.

How does society choose among all the possible points on the accumulation possibility frontier? In the Millian tradition, one might look to individual utility functions, summarized by a set of community indifference curves. Utility, $U = U(F_1, F_2)$, is maximized subject to the limited supply of surplus labor which is available for accumulation at the point F^*. Society decides its time-preference for consumption: how much of its net product is to be saved and invested in more constant capital (F_1), and how much is to go to additional consumption by workers and capitalists (F_2).

In a capitalist economy, the decision to invest depends on the rate of interest. As Irving Fisher and his disciples have explained, both the rate of interest and the amount of investment depend on the opportunities to invest income and the impatience to spend it. The amount of investment depends on the willingness of potential savers to postpone consumption. It is here that class concepts are relevant. For no matter how neutral our language, it is clear that given the technical alternatives the decision to invest is largely in the hands of the capitalists unless counteracted by class forces. One can express this elegantly as the income effect in consumption-saving preference functions or more simply the Cambridge assertion that "workers don't save" but the meaning is the same: the decision to invest depends on the rate of interest, which ultimately is the price that capitalists have to be paid to induce them not to transform their property into consumption.

Certainly it is true that workers do, in fact, save and could save more if they chose to restrict consumption expenditure. It is not by their legal relations to the means of production, as employees, that workers do not control the rate of saving. Contrary to Marx it is the social conditioning which is the ultimate determinant of class behavioral patterns. Regardless of the ultimate source of working class consciousness Marx is justified in identifying labor as a group and he is entitled to speak in favor of its interests. Marx's second objection to capitalism is that the imputation of social cost to private property gives the owners of the means of production a decisive role in determining the growth pattern of the economy.

In Kaldor's view, the decisions of the capitalists to invest in constant capital rather than enlarge the wages fund determines the division of national income into profits and wages. Marx would insist that these decisions are not made by individuals but by antagonistic classes which oppose each other in a "bilateral monopoly" situation more aptly analyzed by the theory of games than equilibrium economics.

This approach avoids the anomalies in defining the quantity of capital in order to calculate its marginal product, which plague modern capital theorists. Physically, one cannot compare an engine lathe with a tree directly. They are made commensurable only through the income they earn. The strand in Marx's analysis we are pursuing would suggest that the income of the capitalist class might not depend on the catalog of assets they own, but on their actions as a more or less cohesive group viz-a-viz the proletarians who *also* are physically heterogeneous. His discussion of the "fetishism of commodities" suggests that the difficulties of traversing from micro- to macroeconomics have been exaggerated by the attempt to aggregate the productivities and utilities of unlike *things*. The concept of class bargaining implies that the divisions of consumption and investment of familiar macroeconomics are not properly the aggregation of disparate products or consumer propensities, but the interaction of macrosocial entities—classes.

Microeconomic calculations by individuals—consumers or capitalists—are relevant when the marginal quantities are proximate substitutes for each other, and in a practical sense can be made homogeneous. But this is true for a comparatively small range of products. When the individual *acts* as part of a class ·and identifies with group goals, then the class must first get its share of the national product, and then the individuals must be resolved within the overall framework.

I do not wish to overstate this argument. Often Marx reasoned as a determinist. Then, like every other classical economist, he determined the working-class income as the sum of the values of the individual labor-power given by the labor technically required to produce worker subsistence. But when he became an active labor agitator—and it will be remembered that he was a practicing revolutionary throughout his life—he insisted on the possibility of increasing the wages fund and labor's relative share. Subsistence was an historically defined term. The workers' share in national income can be increased without inflation by decreasing the percentage of surplus value which goes to the capitalists. The Marxian model of capitalism may be most meaningfully completed, or closed, by taking the

27

relative strengths of opposing classes as the parameter defining the operation of the system. (Wolfson, ch. 3) The chief difference between the Marxian and Keynesian system is in this closure. In the latter it is the demand for investment which is decisive. Investment depends on the "desired" capital-output ratio, which in turn depends on what Joan Robinson calls the "animal spirits" of the capitalists.

If Keynes made us wiser, he also made us a bit sadder. He showed how capitalism could be maintained at full employment, regardless of structural problems of conflicts of classes, races, and oligopolistic market structures. The macroeconomic medicine Keynes prescribed has fostered compromise which is not optimal to each class. This can be seen by superimposing both labor and capitalist accumulation possibility frontiers on each other. In Marxian terms the frontier is the total surplus *labor* directly and indirectly used in accumulating F_1 and F_2. Capitalists weigh labor differently in order to equalize the rate of profit. The capitalist frontier will be *national income* at market prices equal to the money value of inputs by all factors of production.

Suppose we carry the analysis out in Keynesian terms to relate to familiar macroeconomic concepts. National income (Y) is either consumed (E) or invested (I) in terms of the *prices of production* which are obtainable on the capitalist market. Labor (or any other group), which weights these inputs differently from the capitalist market, would attach a different set of coefficients to E and I. The capitalist frontier is thus $Y = E + I$. The labor frontier is $aY = bE + cI$ or, dividing by a, $Y = \alpha E + \beta I$.

In the consumption-investment plane, the capitalist frontier is a straight line with a negative slope of $45°$. The labor frontier may lie completely within or beyond the capitalist frontier, it may coincide with the capitalist frontier, or it may intersect the frontier. Only the last case is relevant to full employment. Any point beyond either frontier implies more sacrifice than a class is able or willing to make and hence represents an unbearable situation. A point within a frontier represents less than full employment of labor or capital. If the labor frontier lies beyond the capitalist frontier, then either labor is unemployed or capital must accept an intolerable situation. *Mutatis mutandis*, if the labor frontier lies within the capitalist frontier, labor must make sacrifices or capital is unemployed. In the case where the frontiers coincide, the classes value labor and property in exactly the same proportion. This would not be the case except in the rare eventuality that all industries had the same organic composition of capital so that prices of production equaled values. We may neglect this possibility since there is no tendency to equalization.

We need only examine the case where the lines intersect shown in Figure 2. The horizontally lined region is unbearable to labor, and the vertically marked region is unbearable to capital. The cross-hatched region is unacceptable to both, while the borders of the triangular-shaped wedges which meet at point B are satisfactory to one group and not the other. The interior of the white region embodying points such as A is bearable in the sense that it does not require more effort than can be exerted, but it is unsatisfactory since it is a condition of unemployed labor and capital.

Only point B represents full employment and bearable social costs on both criteria. In general B will not be optimal to both classes. Workers maximizing their own utility with indifference curves similar to (iii) will choose C. Capitalists maximizing with indifference curves like (ii) will choose D. Interestingly, if both classes have the *same* indifference map such as (i) they will still not agree to choose B since the slopes of both frontiers differ at that point and so cannot be tangent to the same curve. Only in the very special case where workers and capitalists have different indifference curve systems whose slope just equals that of their respective frontiers at B is there a basis for class agreement in the form of capital accumulation and consumption.

FIGURE 2

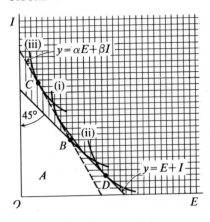

What we say here about the dissatisfaction of a two-class society, can be enlarged to include a multi-group system. Nobody is likely to be satisfied. Alas, a generation of Keynesian liberals fought so hard for a macroeconomic guarantee of full employment, and their children are grossly discontent with what they have wrought. The question has become: Whose utility function is to be maximized?

The decision to accumulate capital in constant instead of variable form amounts to a postponement of consumption by the workers in favor of a future flow of income by more productive "round-about" methods. To make a decision now about the future requires that the present value of future income be calculated by some rate of discount. If one were to accept the Marxian class value judgments, then this calculation ought to be made at the workers' rate of discount.

The dynamic issue which differentiates capitalism from socialism, and remains the essential issue for Marxism after a century of criticism, is still which *class* determines the direction and rate of accumulation. In pure market capitalism, the discount rate is expressed in a decentralized, microeconomic, market rate of interest. In the absence of government fiscal and monetary policy, it reflects the productivity of capital and the time preference of the capitalists. In the socialist economy, where all the growth decisions are made centrally, the authorities establish a rate of interest which presumably reflects the workers' rate of discount. The socialist firm has no legal option to convert its capital equipment into articles of consumption. Rather it will employ constant capital up to the point where its marginal product equals the rate of interest assigned by the planning authorities. "Mixed capitalism" might not be as antithetical to the socialist model as the continuing private ownership of property might suggest. Thoroughgoing macroeconomic control of the economy often implies an administered interest rate. Should the accumulation policy of private firms prove to be interest-inelastic, direct fiscal expenditure of the government is used to achieve the accumulation plan.

Whether this development is sinister or benevolent depends on political consideration. In *The New Industrial State*, John Galbraith has lately warned of the hazards of the influence of the military-industrial "technostructure" on the plan. But since he, more than many others, has been an advocate of such planning, it can hardly be the existence of the plan to which he objects. Rather, it is that the plan does not suit his preferences, and seems to be unduly based on the utility functions of elite groups which he feels can only be tenuously connected with ownership of the means of production or membership in the working class. Clearly, the more highly planned an economic system is, the more complex and political becomes the conflicts that determine the effective rate of surplus value. Class and caste, national ambitions and anxieties, interact in complex dynamic patterns which can not be neatly excluded from consideration.

If ownership is operationally separated from control of industrial enterprises, the question becomes which group of bureaucrats—for better or worse—decides what will be regarded as social cost or social welfare. The sales-maximizing management of the oligopolistic firm that has figured so prominently in economic literature in recent years is hardly to be distinguished from the Soviet efforts to "overfulfil the plan." The mere presence or absence of private property does not determine which, if any, ownership class will determine the present versus future planning decisions. If stockholders can own without controlling the "capitalist" firm, the planning authorities can control without owning the "socialist" enterprise.

At best, Marx's legal definition of economic systems in terms of ownership is obsolete because it tends to make the choice between alternative systems an all-or-none bargain between private or public ownership of productive property. Rather, the issue is which property incomes are to be considered social costs. The important question is determining the social welfare function as the "general will" by the political process, more than in planning to optimize it.

Would it be possible to imagine a socialist society without accepting some degree of social cost imputed to the use of property? Obvious counter examples come to mind whose importance has grown since Marx wrote:

1. *Consumers' capital.* The *Communist Manifesto* did not propose the nationalization of personal property in the form of consumer durables. Income, Marx's materialism suggested, was a flow of material commodities produced by labor working with the means of production. Hence, Marx did not object to the flow of satisfactions to the owners of consumer durables which result from exclusive control over these stocks of wealth. But if the satisfaction of ownership is important in the workers' income, the sacrifice of this property must be considered as a social cost even to a society without capitalists. Evidently the Soviet public is making this cost increasingly evident to the planners. Cheap public transportation and low-rent tenements are imperfect substitutes for owning a car and house.

2. *Human capital.* The claim to future income by the owners of stored-up labor is not limited to physical capital. Marx considered that the capitalist system tended to reduce labor to simple unskilled labor by the extension of the assembly-line fractionalization of jobs into the most elementary operations. Consequently, economic growth was limited by the increase in the numbers of the labor force, and the accumulation of constant capital. Current evidence contradicts Marx's prejudice that only the latter embodied technical change. Individuals may react to the productivity of human capital by investing in themselves. It is a current commonplace for a future-oriented young man to express his Puritanism by getting a Ph.D. to enter the elite, unlike Horatio Alger who went into business and saved more tangible assets. Where returns to physical capital are illegal, as in the Soviet Union, or stunted, as in the former colonial African nations, inordinate efforts are made to enter the bureaucracy. It is unclear to what extent the salaries of these elite groups are returns to their product-

ivity rather than transfers from productive sectors; yet their income has nothing to do with ownership of the means of production.

3. *Workers save.* While we have found it expedient to provisionally identify workers' income with consumption, this is only a first approximation in advanced countries. To the extent that workers' savings are utilized in the construction of physical capital, their supply price for the savings will have some influence on the growth rate. Insofar as saving is accomplished through taxation to finance public investment, the workers' political influence is significant. Certainly Marx's legal formulation of classes and social systems is unduly rigid, and more so now than in Marx's day when administrators came almost exclusively from capitalist circles. But it is foolish to ignore his central message: Basic decisions in capitalist society are collective rather than individual. They are made in many cases under circumstances in which an optimal judgment cannot be made which will maximize the welfare of the whole community. Consequently, welfare and growth are the product of class conflict and the balance of power. Contemporary planned societies bring this conflict overtly into the political arena where the imputation of value to human and physical property becomes indistinct and intermingled with national and bureaucratic motivations. The more blurred the distinction becomes, the more indistinct becomes the separation between capitalism and socialism. The public sector grows, and as the size of private interests approximates that of the state, they take on state-like functions.

3. MARX'S ACCOUNT OF ECONOMIC GROWTH

We have seen that Marx's working class criticism of capitalism has two dimensions: its choice of technique and the rate of accumulation of capital toward the technology chosen. He is concerned with goals and growth paths. In the critically important central portion of *Capital* (Volume I, Parts 3, 4), Marx uses the nineteenth-century British experience to document his theoretical indictment of capitalism. These chapters depend very little on the labor theory of value as a positive theory of exchange. Rather, the argument hinges on the difference between social cost and the market valuations of capitalism.

Despite its accumulation of constant capital in amounts far in excess of previous stages of society, Marx argues that the technology chosen by capitalism is still excessively labor intensive. *To the capitalist*, the alternative production cost to constant capital is labor-power, while the gross *social* cost, on Marx's norm, is the labor expended by the workers. A rational firm will accumulate value in labor-power up to the point where its (marginal) product equals that of an equal increase in value of constant capital. Since the social cost of a good exceeds the market compensation to workers for their labor-power by the amount of surplus labor, labor-power tends to be overaccumulated. Labor-power, Marx says, is "squandered." Capitalism tends to husband its material capital but waste and abuse its human resources.

This is perfectly rational from the point of view of the capitalist firm, but, labor tends to be undervalued when income is imputed to capital. Just as Ricardo argued that land, though scarce, is the "free gift of nature," Marx insists that capital is a socially free legacy of man's history as a productive being. Marx addresses the reader who "is imbued with capitalist notions" and therefore "will naturally miss here the 'interest' that the machine, in proportion to its capital value, adds to the product. It is, however, easily seen that since a machine no more creates new value than any other part of constant capital, it cannot add any value under the name 'interest' . . . .

The capitalist mode of calculating which appears *prima facie* absurd, and repugnant to the laws of the creation of value, will be explained in the third book of this work." (*Capital*, I, 425n.)

Marx describes the efforts of the capitalists to economize on constant capital at the expense of the workers. Since they own their machines they are careful in their operation to avoid damage; but they only purchase the flow of labor-power and are not individually concerned with the preservation of the stock of human capital. The firm which did not optimize its production in the capitalist manner could not survive competition. Marx suggests that early factory safety legislation and protection of female and child labor by the state are simply the capitalist class reaction to what in present jargon is called "the external cost of the use of human inputs."

In the same vein, Marx discusses the large interest cost to the capitalist firm of its stock of constant capital. It is the "capitalist mode of calculating" to combine constant capital with as much cheap labor-power as is profitable. The machines must never be idle. Moreover, in a period of rapid technological advance, such as the industrial revolution in England, it is imperative that the capitalist make a very nice calculation of the possibilities of intensive use of means of production. The alternative is bankruptcy, for the rapid rate of obsolescence, by shortening the time required to recover fixed costs, enlarges the necessary gross rate of interest.

Marx cries out at the suffering and degradation of the working class that results. Following Engels' earlier study, he explores the physical, moral, and educational debilitation of the proletarians with excruciating thoroughness. He rings all the changes of overwork, dangerous occupations, night work, unhealthful conditions, malnutrition, and miserable housing.

Marx does not consider the possibility of the social value

of labor to be systematically underestimated, and yet the labor force to consist of highly skilled, high-wage labor complementary to complex machinery. This was a subsequent development. The early stage of the industrial revolution was more akin to economic development with unlimited amounts of low productivity labor. The technology of this stage was adapted to the labor force, and, by the impoverishment of the workers, tended to keep them in an unskilled condition. Given the labor force, there was no motivation for change *internal to the firm*.

This first stage, which corresponds to the path of economic growth envisioned by W.A. Lewis, was dubbed "manufacture" by Marx. It consisted in technological change through the process of division of labor rather than through the introduction of power machinery. Each operation was simplified and routinized, so that the artisan became reduced to unskilled labor. In a characteristic formulation, Marx argues that labor is transformed by the manufacture stage of industrialization into simple, unskilled, homogeneous labor. The theoretical problem of reducing actual concrete labors to an abstract homogeneous unit which plagues the labor theory of value is identified with the historical process in which the differences in types and productivities of labor are diminished.

Machinery is introduced only when an increment in output to each firm can be achieved at lower cost by an increment of constant capital than of variable capital, even though the social opportunity cost is total labor expended. "In England", he remarks, "women are still occasionally used instead of horses for hauling canal boats, because the labor required to produce horses and machines is an accurately known quantity, while that required to maintain the women of the surplus population is below all calculation. Hence, nowhere do we find a more shameful squandering of human labor-power for the most despicable purposes than in England, the land of machinery." (*Cap-ital*, V I, 430)

But the manufacturing stage comes to an end and is replaced by "Machinery and Modern Industry." Internal migration from country to the towns is completed and the population does not grow rapidly enough to maintain the labor force in infinitely elastic supply at subsistence wages. The working class reacts to the barbarous conditions of manufacture by agitating for a shorter workday, higher wages, and for the limitation of child and female labor. The returns to labor get closer to their social cost, although Marx would insist that *any* profit return to capital was socially unwarranted. The result is the replacement of living labor by constant capital.

Marx could only view this as a positive development. It is part of man's constant struggle to subdue nature by more effective labor. Yet the tempo at which the mechanization process occurs, he says, is the product of class antagonistic conditions. The first wave of mechanization causes long hours of low-wage simple labor to be replaced by intensified work. A higher degree of attention and skill as well as extra effort is required. Marx regarded both skill and effort as multipliers of social cost. He could not imagine that the degree of skill and education necessary for labor in modern production could reduce the disutility of highly skilled labor to the point where given the choice, some individuals prefer to accumulate their own human capital rather than material wealth.

Marx was also saying that the changeover is too rapid although the goals are too modest. Despite the demand for labor in the machine building industries, involuntary technological unemployment results; wages are driven down by the replenishment of the "industrial reserve army of unemployed." Ultimately, this reflects the difference in technologies and accumulation plans desired by the two classes. The workers are anxious to reduce hours of labor and to severely limit the participation of children in the work force at the expense of the income which they might earn if they continued on with the new technology as they had with the old. This is a feature of socialist as well as capitalist economies. Yet, it is clearly not in labor's interest to accept rates of investment that will unduly limit consumption and hence its share in real income—perhaps to the extent of unemployment or reduced real wages. From the capitalist point of view, the desire for investment is given by their own "animal spirits" and the anticipation of profit.

Thus we have a distinctive combination of criticism of capitalism. Each class, Marx is telling us, has its own target technology; and for each target, each class has a different growth path toward it. The technology chosen by capital is too labor intensive. In its early stages, capitalism involves large-scale exploitation of cheap labor. In Marx's view, because of the undervaluation of labor it never does sufficiently attempt to replace human effort by mechanical innovations. But once having found a profitable opportunity to accumulate in constant capital, the investment traverse to a more capital intensive technology may be too rapid. The resulting technological unemployment and depressed wages is the "increasing misery of the proletariat," which Marx considered to be the "general law of capitalist accumulation."

Strata of the working class around the world continue to be beset with the process Marx described. They are inducted into the labor force in unskilled labor-intensive production and then are discarded by technical change. Thus, if one were to describe the symptoms of the Negro ghetto in the United States, they would be strikingly similar to Marx and Engels' description of the condition of the working class in Britain:

internal migration from country to town, employment in menial labor-intensive industry, miserable housing, degrading labor which tends to undermine familial relationships, inadequate education and demoralization of the youth, the appearance of a *lumpenproletariat*, technological unemployment as advanced methods of production dispense with unskilled labor, and the ultimate growth of a militant spirit of rebellion.

This picture of the lowest strata of the American working class can be writ large to include the conditions of the working class in the slums surrounding the cities in underdeveloped nations. Agricultural labor was brought into production for the market in both peasant and plantation agriculture, and then transformed into a surplus population by the lessened world dependence on labor-intensive tropical produce and the shift in profitability to advanced mechanized production in all countries. No less pitiable is the derivative situation of redundant workers drawn to the terrible ghettos in the cities by the distress in agriculture. This disfunction of surplus unskilled labor is epidemic around the world.

Marx's famous discussion of the "increasing misery" of the workers emphasizes stratification of the labor force. When Marx attempts to extend his correct description of the lowest strata left behind by mechanization to the working class as a whole, the argument falters.

The lowest sediment of the relative surplus-population finally dwells in the sphere of pauperism. Exclusive of vagabonds, criminals, prostitutes, in a word the "dangerous" classes, this layer of society consists of three categories. First, those able to work. One need only glance superficially at the statistics of English pauperism to find that the quantity of paupers increases with every crisis, and diminishes with every revival of trade. Second, orphans and pauper children. These are candidates for the industrial reserve-army, and are, in times of great prosperity . . . speedily and in large numbers enrolled in the active army of labourers. Third, the demoralized and ragged, and those unable to work, chiefly people who succumb to their incapacity for adaptation due to the division of labour; people who have passed the normal age of the labourer; the victims of industry, whose number increases with the increase of dangerous machinery, of mines, chemical works, &c., the mutilated, the sickly, the widows &c. Pauperism is the hospital of the active labour-army and the dead weight of the industrial reserve army. [*Capital*, I, 706-7]

Marx then goes on to argue that "The greater the social wealth . . . the greater is the industrial reserve army" by an appeal to a mechanical analogy, "The relative mass of the industrial reserve army increases with the potential energy of wealth." This assertion cannot be universally justified and the thunderous denunciation of capitalism ends in an equivocation: "The more extensive . . . the lazarus-layers of the working-class and the industrial reserve army, the greater is official pauperism. *This is the absolute general law of capitalist accumulation.* Like all other laws it is modified in its working by many circumstances, the analysis of which does not concern us here." (*Ibid.*)

4. MARX'S POSITIVE POLITICAL ECONOMY

When we decided in this essay to follow Marx's analysis of the circulation of commodities and labor rather than discuss the labor theory of value as an explanation of price, we committed ourselves to Marx the militant labor reformer rather than Marx the revolutionist. We translated from labor to money flows by means of prices of production. The closure of the system by the rate of surplus value rather than subsistence wage meant that we would arrive at conclusions in "relative" rather than "absolute" terms. We discussed the relative shares of capital and labor in the national product, not the physical amount of product, the amount of labor embodied in a single commodity. Wages were not determined by the subsistence basket of groceries, but by labor's per capita share in the national product. We could not know if that share meant a bowl of rice and a shred of fish, or an automobile and a color TV since we did not have any production function to relate labor and capital inputs to fish and television outputs. We examined Marxian macroeconomics rather than microeconomics. I think that it is rather good macroeconomics because it is frankly stated in class terms and avoids the circumlocutions of propensities and illusions, which Keynes inflicted upon us.

Does our conclusion that the working class has a social value system of its own commit it to revolution? Only if social values are so far apart that tolerable compromise is impossible. Compromise is easier if the absolute level of income is higher, and if, as we have suggested, neither class really could function strictly within its own value system. Social revolution would then be a matter of conscious, deliberate political decision as much as collective human action can ever be. That would never do for Marx the revolutionist although the younger humanistic Marx might well have embraced this voluntaristic doctrine and grown up to become either a parlor radical or a workaday pork-chop unionist.

Ever since he wrote the *Theses on Feuerbach*, Marx argued that individuals did not make the decisions between alternative goals. The objective process of history established the norms of society. Marx thought that he had demonstrated that: 1) labor is exploited by the very workings of the capitalist system; 2) the misery of the workers will tend to increase over time, ultimately driving them to rebellion; 3) capitalism will cease to function due to the internal contradictions in the system itself; and 4) these processes are not the result of the good or bad will of the capitalists or workers, and are beyond their power to reverse.

The link-pin in Marxian theory of exploitation is the assertion that under capitalism commodities exchange in proportion to the total labor embodied in their production. Then the value of labor-power is its subsistence, and the surplus value is the unearned income accruing to capital. As we have seen, differences in organic composition of capital make the labor theory of value true only for an ideal socialist society, not characteristic of capitalism, but we put this aspect aside.

The labor theory of value fails to identify Marx's normative views about social cost with the facts of the capitalist economy because he attempts to use a macroeconomic concept of a single homogeneous input to do the work of microeconomic analysis. When one attempts to relate physical input to outputs, it becomes evident that both of these categories are *inhomogeneous*. A *macroeconomic* analysis must use a single input by its very need to sum up human activities. Once the choice of social system is made the input is given: for Marx it was labor and for Keynes it was money.

In microeconomic analysis, the valuations of economic activity depend very much on how much of each activity is chosen. Choice is central to the determination of the technology of an economy because human preferences determine production as much as the material relations of production determine human behavior. If one attempts to use a macroeconomic concept for microeconomic purposes, as Marx does, then the problem of choice vanishes because it has been defined away by aggregation. If there were a single factor of production, and if each industry produced a single product (no joint products), and if there are constant returns to the single scarce input, then *one* best production set of activities will be chosen. The various combinations of the final products which society decides to produce will have no effect on the rate of product substitution. A best technology would be chosen and relative prices would be constant along a production possibility frontier. Indeed consumer choice will be irrelevant to the theory of value. The reader will recognize this assertion as Samuelson's "substitution theorem."

FIGURE 3

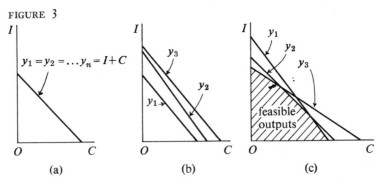

The moral is that macroeconomics is not a theory of *exchange* value. Marx knew that actual production of physical goods requires many *kinds* of labor as well as other factors. The result is a system of *many* constraints. There are three possibilities, displayed in Figure 3, for two physical goods x and y. Only if all of the factor inputs are identically specialized to the production of any of the final products the frontiers they comprise will all be parallel straight lines and, as in Figure 3a, they may also coincide. In this case we can talk of a single composite physical input such as simple homogeneous labor. The factors may be differently specialized, but one will be the innermost, and it will be the sole effective scarce factor. The others will be redundant as in Figure 3b. These two cases require an incredible coincidence. The only relevant case is Figure 3c, where the input frontiers intersect. Since the feasible production possibility region lies within *all* the frontiers simultaneously, it must be convex. Consequently, the amount of one product which has to be given up to get more of another, the slope of the frontier, depends on how much of it is used. It follows that one way or another, society has to decide on how much it will be willing to give up of all other products to get an additional amount of any one of them. Demand as well as supply determines price, whether that demand is expressed as individual choices on the market, or collective private or governmental desires.

In partial equilibrium terms we say that demand is irrelevant to the determination of value only if supply shows constant returns to scale. (Wolfson, pp. 60, 63) In Figure 4a, the labor per unit product is invariant if labor is the sole scarce input, or if labor and other inputs are used in fixed proportions so that no factors are specialized. (Or if fortuitous economies of scale precisely counterbalance diminishing returns to the scarce factors.) Given this infinitely elastic supply curve, a shift in demand due to changes in tastes and incomes would determine the amount of the product that is "socially necessary" (e.g., Q_1, Q_2, Q_3), but would not alter the content (OW) of each unit produced. The subjective element of choice would be irrelevant; value would be determined by the technical coefficients of production.

There are difficulties with this explanation. As a student of Ricardo, Marx was aware that some firms operate under conditions of greater or less than average costs, even in the very long run, and consequently the industry faced other than horizontal supply curves. It will not do to argue that supply price is *approximately* constant in the long run. First of all, it may not be constant, and secondly, it is not much of an "essence" which is only 93 percent pure. (Stigler)

The case of increasing costs is represented in Figure 4b by the supply function SS'. Long-run price W_1 would be determined at the margin of demand and supply. The supply function is the sum of the marginal cost curves of each firm.

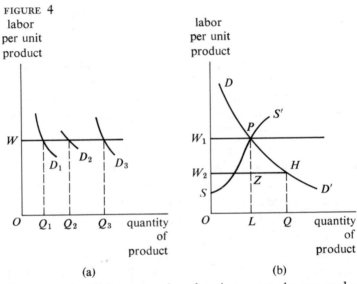

FIGURE 4

(a)

(b)

Consequently, if labor were the sole private cost, the area under the supply curve, $OSPL$, would represent the total labor expended on this product. But the sum of the values is the rectangle $OLPW_1$, leaving a systematic difference which can only be attributed to nonlabor factors. Actually this difference, SPW_1 is Marshall's "producer's surplus"; in our discussion it is the difference between the amount of labor society actually has to expend, the area under SS', and the amount of labor it would be willing to spend, $OLPW_1$.

46

Marx can, and occasionally does, make value the amount of labor society is *willing* to expend as socially necessary labor. I have suggested in *A Reappraisal of Marxian Economics* (ch. 3) that by so doing, Marx made labor a creature of *demand* rather than supply. If, as often appears in his writing, he had a unit elastic demand curve in mind rather than an infinitely elastic supply curve, it might be possible to distinguish value from price. *Value* is the labor society is willing to expend on a product, equal to *any* rectangle subtended under DD'. Market *price* is P, the labor embodied at the margin. The total labor expended is $OSPL$ drawn equal to OW_2ZL. W_2 would be the labor per unit product using the production techniques which give rise to SS'. Were goods sold at their average values, W_2, society would still be *willing* to expend the same total labor on these commodities as it does when they are sold at their prices, P or W_1. Were goods sold at their values but produced under SS', then the producer's surplus SPW_1 would reappear as the rectangle of equal area, $LQHZ$.

On this interpretation, value is a *fund of labor* society allocates to a commodity and not a long-run price. Values change as a *shift* in the demand curve rather than a movement along it. Marx often speaks of there being so much "room" on the market for any commodity. Labor value then becomes an historically conditioned, subjective choice by the *superstructure* of society about the *proportion* of its social cost it is willing to use for any particular purpose. (Ward) It is ideological and not material. If Marx is to avoid inconsistency, labor in its social aspect must be considered subject to human *decision* as we have been suggesting earlier in this essay.

The demand for apples or teacups is hardly a social fund devoted to their production. Marx centered his attention on the value of one commodity, labor-power, the amount of labor society allocates to the reproduction of the laborers. Marx defines this as the subsistence of the workers but hastens to add that subsistence is a variable and historically defined term. It may be understood either as a constant subsistence supply price or as demand for labor embodied in a wages fund of subsistence goods. Despite his charge of eclecticism against Mill, Marx also held several theories of value and often reserved the fund theory for labor but did not distinguish it from the cost of production theory as explicitly as Mill. The verbal expression of these two explanations can be made almost identical, and in certain historical circumstances they were not contradictory. The conditions of the early manufacturing stage of the industrial revolution in Britain were effectively of unlimited supplies of labor. The supply curve of labor was horizontal, very close to the biological level of subsistence. Either definition of value would do under these circumstances. Men, women and children worked long hours in the frightful mills to provide family subsistence. The labor force pressed against the wages fund and reduced wage rates to subsistence.

As the process of industrialization proceeded, the supply curve of labor-power had ceased to be horizontal. By the time the first volume of *Capital* appeared (1867), the migration of labor to the cities was largely completed. Workers reduced the length of the working day through legislation and direct action. Child and female labor were regulated. Wage rates increased, so that the description "subsistence wages" was either false or had to be fudged into meaninglessness as "historically relative." If the labor theory of value were to be applied, it had to be interpreted in our second sense of a social allocation of labor to the production of labor-power, a wages fund.

Marx was quick to reject Mill's notion that a wages fund implied an iron law of wages. The fund was not determined technically by the stock of "corn," but by class struggle. Capitalists and workers were in a complex political and economic bilateral conflict situation over their shares in national income. The rate of surplus value was the index to the state of that struggle and was the parameter which determined the growth characteristics of the economy.

I conclude that the value of labor-power may only be consistently thought of as the amount of social effort that accrues to the workers. The absolute wage rate as the output of subsistence is not available to Marxian economics. Only the relative share of the national product that goes to labor can be known. Constancy of relative shares appears in "bourgeois" microeconomics as the derived demand for labor which is implied in the unit elasticities for both labor and capital in the Cobb-Douglas production function:

$$Q = AL^{\alpha}K^{\beta} \qquad \text{(For constant returns to scale } \alpha + \beta = 1\text{)}$$

L and K are labor and capital in physical units, Q represents physical output, and A is a constant of proportionality reflecting the "state of the technical arts." Paul Douglas developed this function in order to explain the puzzling long-term stickiness of the relative shares of labor and capital in the national product of developed nations. On the basis of marginal productivity theory, he showed that each factor would have a constant share in the national product. If the wage rate rose, employment would fall proportionally, so that the share of labor income would be α. J. R. Hicks described this situation as unit elasticity of substitution of labor and capital.

In Marxian terms, the rate of surplus value is β/α. With more temerity than wisdom we rename the Cobb-Douglas function the Constant Rate of Surplus Value Function (CRS). If labor is withheld at low wages or because of preferences for shorter work days and the limitation of the labor of women and children, then constant capital is substituted for living labor. As long as the process remains on the CRS function, class income is unchanged.

What determines α and β? Douglas suggested that the function represented a technological relationship. Production of each firm took place at the limit of its production possibilities given by the state of the engineering arts. Hence, factor shares were ultimately a technological fact. This is not very satisfying. Perhaps, for practical analysis, a single firm may be considered to take the state of the arts as virtually known. But, when one aggregates to the economy as a whole and contemplates long run changes, it is very difficult to say that all the possible ways of producing all the possible things "exist" in a production function. (Leibenstein) The assertion has a truly Leibnizian metaphysical ring, for if such a function exists, did not potential production processes always exist? What might we mean by new knowledge? If a function of production possibilities exists, can any society really approach its frontiers? Can the frontiers be known?

The underlying data in production analysis are the facts of constancy of relative shares or actual inputs and outputs, not a direct inspection of the unobservable aggregate production function of *maximum* outputs. One might just as easily interpret the observations as caused by class collective bargaining over relative shares in the long run. Perhaps α and β are socially determined and the technology *introduced* into production reflects the bargaining strength of the opposing classes. Then the CRS function represents factor combinations along a line of class truce which tends to persist for long periods of time since underlying class attitudes and the structure of the ruling technology in advanced nations tends to change only slowly. The rapid technical change which accompanies *social* upheavals—think of wartime innovations—makes the second interpretation of the CRS function more appealing.

If the demand for labor depends on cumulative changes in ideology and accumulated means of production which is economic history, what of supply? The shifting of the worker's supply function from infinite wage-elasticity at low levels of subsistence income as income rises makes it clear that we are dealing with historically evolved worker attitudes rather than material causation.

Can Marx really say that labor is exploited? Can Paul Douglas deny it? Science cannot answer. Certainly under capitalism, labor does not get the whole national product and is prevented from getting it by the substitutability of other factors. The opportunity to make the substitution appears as the marginal productivity of physical assets to the owners of the means of production, and surplus value to Marx's workers. Neither term is more than an epithet which expresses value judgments about the ethic of private property. To make normative human judgments into statements about the objective nature of labor or capital as physical entities is to fall victim to what Marx rightly called the fetishism of commodities. Alas, he fell into the same trap himself!

5. THE COLLAPSE OF CAPITALISM

Social revolutions occur, Lenin commented, only when both the ruling and laboring classes cannot continue on in the old way. (*Left-Wing Communism*) It had to be shown that workers will be increasingly exploited and capitalism would tend to either secular stagnation or increasingly violent recurrent crises. Later critiques of imperialism advanced by Lenin and

Rosa Luxemburg were based on the need to delay an inevitable domestic crisis. The breakdown of capitalism in a closed economy is the major premise of all the Marxian versions of the revolutionary transition to communism.

Marx's dynamic theory is a dilemma model of either excess supply of labor or labor shortage. The first stage of the industrial revolution was identified with the increasing misery of the proletarians as a result of economic development with unlimited supplies of excess labor. The expropriated agricultural population was thrown into labor-intensive manufacturing. In Britain the rate of accumulation of variable capital eventually exceeded the population growth rate. Capitalism entered the second stage of labor shortage. Increasing wages squeezed profits reducing the capitalists' share. Technological "relative overpopulation" replenished the industrial reserve army of unemployed. Periodically when labor-saving change was inadequate, an economic crisis resulted, restoring the necessary labor surplus and the misery of the workers.

Between these extremes, is there not an equilibrium rate of accumulation for constant and variable capital which maintains full employment without changing the relative incomes of labor and capital? Could income grow along an exponential "golden age" path at the "natural rate" of population growth and technical progress? Marx's answer is that as accumulation takes place in constant capital, opposing tendencies are at work. Demand for means of production increases the demand for labor-power as a multiple of itself, and at the same time the constant capital is used as a substitute for labor and tends to reduce the demand for living labor. Marx expected that the short-run growth in demand for labor-power would outrun its supply. (*Capital*, Vol. III ch. 15) The "absolute overproduction of capital" is an anticipation of the Harrod-Domar knife-edge. Captialists' income is given by the sticky rate of surplus value. During the "frenzied" bursts of accumulation, the ratio of the stock of constant capital to output does not change rapidly and the labor supply is exhausted. Declining profit rates halt accumulation and a crisis results through a multiplier reduction in demand for both wage-goods and means of production.

The Marxian model is an even more confining limitation than the Harrod-Domar formulation. Keynesian real income purports to be the net value of physical output measured in constant prices; it may grow indefinitely with technical progress as well as with the labor force. When Marx uses value as a microeconomic term, he is led to identify labor value with the real income return to individuals rather than a *share* in the national product. Hence the sum of all the value that society can produce is fixed by the labor force and the "intensity" with which it works. National product *is* the labor *expended* as an input, not the reflux of products of society. Once full employment has been reached, the gross flow of value cannot be enlarged by technical progress.

Marx realizes that technical change can increase *surplus* value by cheapening the labor required for workers' subsistence. The lower value of labor-power produces "relative surplus value." Yet there is a limit on the surplus value which can be produced—ultimately it cannot exceed the gross hours worked. (*Capital*, III, 295–96) If this surplus value is produced with larger outlays of capital, the *rate* of profit will fall even though the "mass" of surplus value is unchanged. Marx argued that if q increased and σ remained constant, the rate of profit would tend to fall since $R = \sigma (1 - q)$. The development of capitalism, he said, was characterized by increasing organic composition of capital and consequently concluded that the rate of profit would fall.

But in the long run, may not σ rise as well as q? The rate of profit would only fall if the percentage change in the organic composition of capital exceeded the percentage change in the rate of surplus value. The rate of surplus value might rise if the productivity was embodied in the increased organic composition. If the subsistence of the worker takes less and less labor, the rate of surplus value would increase without limit and the rate of profit might rise. Would either labor surplus or labor shortage result?

We can study this problem by starting from the combinations of the factors of production—labor power and constant capital—consistent with a given rate of surplus value. If the constant rate of surplus value condition holds along with the condition that the individual capitalists are free to substitute capital for labor up to the point where the payment to each factor equals its marginal product, then we are dealing with a Cobb-Douglas (CRS) set of production possibilities which could be multiplied by any coefficient of physical productivity. These are not the technical possibilities, but rather those that are consistent with a given balance of class forces.

The CRS function in Figure 5 is drawn with the provisional assumption that output per man is uniquely determined by the capital-labor ratio. Technical progress is put aside. We will show that contrary to his own attack on fetishism of commodities, the existence of a technical limitation to output in the form of a production function is required for Marx to substantiate his dilemma model of capitalist collapse. In this diagram the abcissa, r, is the ratio of *physical* constant capital, K, and labor, L. The ordinate, y, is equal to physical output, Q, per worker. It is not hard to show that output per man increases at a decreasing rate as more and more capital is used per man. Diminishing returns to r cause the CRS function to decrease in slope and approach the horizontal asymptotically.

Dividing the increase in output per man ($\Delta Q/L$) by the increase in capital per man ($\Delta K/L$) we get the slope of the

FIGURE 5

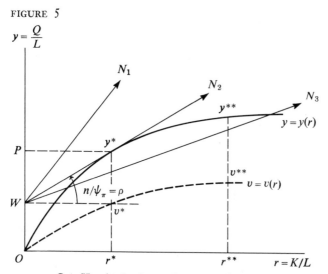

curve $\Delta Q/\Delta K$ which shows how much physical output could be increased by installing another bit of machinery. Under the capitalist rules of the game, this increment in output accrues to the owners of the machinery as the marginal productivity of capital. To Marx it represented the rate of return to the capitalists under conditions of class equilibrium. To the capitalist firm it is the "normal" rate which each individual capitalist has to be paid to get him to allocate his constant capital to a given enterprise. For any r, say r^*, the income of the capitalists per man employed is therefore the slope of the function times r^*.

Labor income per man, the real wage rate, is the balance, OW.

We may divide total product into the labor and capitalist share for each value of r, by drawing the curve v for the real wage. The important property of the CRS function is that the *ratio* of the ordinates of v and y is invariant for all r. That is to say, the factor shares do not change. If labor becomes scarce, capitalists will substitute constant capital for labor by moving from r^* to r^{**}. The real wage *rate* would have risen from v^* to v^{**}; the slope of the y function would decline so the rate of profit falls, but the division of the new product is unchanged. As Marx says, the rate of profit may fall, but the total mass of profit (per man) increases from v^*y^* to $v^{**}y^{**}$.

Now we are able to tackle the problem of the tendency of the rate of profit. Will the capital-labor ratio, like Marx's organic composition of capital, increase indefinitely resulting in a secular decline in the rate of profit? Or, does there exist an equilibrium rate of profit and organic composition for any given CRS function? Does it exist for *every* rate of surplus value? How might such equilibrium be reached?

Marx would employ a classical saving function in which the accumulation of capital comes only from the profits of the capitalists. The percentage of accumulation in constant capital is the capitalists' propensity to save, ψ_π, times the rate of profit on the stock of constant capital, ρ. Now if an equilibrium capital-labor ratio has been achieved, the rate of growth of constant capital accumulation must equal the rate of growth of the labor force, n. Hence, $n = \psi_\pi \rho$, and $\rho = n/\psi_\pi$. The rate of profit on constant capital, ρ, is nothing but the slope of the CRS function at a point; equilibrium occurs when the slopes are equal, and a rap of slope n/ψ_π emanating from W in Figure 5 is tangent to the CRS function. The slope of ray N_2 is such an equilibrium rate of profit which leads to steady growth with capital-labor ratio, r^*, output per man, y^*, and real wages, v^*.

Now how is such an equilibrium rate of profit reached? Consider, first, the disequilibrium ray N_3. Suppose we provisionally take the natural population rate of growth and the propensity to save by the capitalists as exogenous facts of demography and of "bourgeois psychology," and the CRS function as given by embedded technology. Then the slope of the ray through W and the CRS function is known. If ρ, the slope of the CRS function at r^* exceeds n/ψ_π, then the rate of accumulation of constant capital will exceed the natural rate of growth of the labor force and the capital-labor ratio will rise. (Symbolically, if $n/\psi_\pi < \rho$, then $n < \psi_\pi\rho$ and r^* will increase.) The resultant increase in r along the CRS curve will lower the rate of profit and increase total output per man, y. Since the new increased y must be divided in the same proportion as the old between capital and labor, both the points W and P will slide up the vertical axis. The declining slope of the CRS curve will be closer to n/ψ_π until equilibrium is restored at some value of r where N_3 is tangent to the function.

Not only is this an equilibrium, but this is an *optimal* solution in the sense that it gives the maximum output per man which can be achieved for the CRS function. Furthermore, the smaller the slope of N_3, the greater that optimum output will be. Consequently, if the capitalists invest all of the income they do not accumulate in labor-power, ψ_π is at a maximum (unity), and y will also be maximized. If the tendency of the rate of profit to fall is viewed properly as a long-run optimizing problem, it is not a catastrophe. It is simply the adaptation of technology to the long-run parameters of growth: the rate of increase of the population (n), the state of the class struggle (σ), and the willingness of the capitalists to postpone their consumption (ψ_π).

Complete adjustment is not always feasible in the short run. Institutional monetary constraints, like Keynes's liquidity trap, may make the equilibrium profit rate less than the money rate of interest. Marx too held a monetary short-run theory of interest which also set a lower limit on the acceptable rate of profit in the short run. (*Capital*, Vol. III, Part V). In the long run, Marx insisted that since interest represented a subdivision of surplus value, the rate of interest must follow the tendency of the rate of profit. Nevertheless, since Marx viewed the tendency of the rate of profit to decline as central to his critique of capitalism, it is likely that he really did not envision an infinitesimally small interest rate such as would necessitate the "euthanasia of the rentier." The long-run limits on the market rate of interest in money or "own" terms remain a moot point for economists. We can conclude that the ability of capitalism to avoid recurrent depressions and stagnation depends on three open questions of fact: 1) How low is the equilibrium rate of profit? 2) Is there a long-run liquidity trap? If so, how high is the associated interest rate? and 3) What forces tend to change the equilibrium rate of profit?

The other branch of the Marxian dilemma is represented by ray N_1. If the population growth rate is large enough, and the capitalist propensity to save is small enough, there may be *no* point of tangency of N_1 with the CRS curve. That is to say, if $n/\psi_\pi > \rho$ for *all* r, then $n > \rho\psi_\pi$. This means that the labor force grows faster than the accumulation of constant capital, and the capital-labor ratio falls. If all of the labor force were employed, output per man, y, and real wages, v, would also decline toward zero as a result of the fall in r. In Marx's words, labor-power would be "squandered." Since Malthusian checks set biological lower limits on real wages, unemployment would accompany low wage, labor-intensive production.

The picture we have drawn is Marx's nightmare world of the manufacturing stage of the industrial revolution and our contemporary "third world" of the Negro ghetto and the underdeveloped nations. In England of the last century, Marx was able to take the growth of the urban proletariat as the consequence of a once-for-all shift of labor from country to town; but today in *addition*, high population growth rates in underdeveloped nations perpetuate the surplus population. Marx simply assumed the parsimony of the bourgeoisie, but in the former colonial areas the recipients of nonlabor incomes do not readily accumulate their incomes in industrial enterprises. The transition to the labor shortage situation is not nearly as natural or inevitable as it appeared to Marx in Victorian England. The lowest Lazarus-layer of the proletariat continues to suffer increasing misery in our times.

Curiously, both the labor shortage and the labor surplus horns of the dilemma require the same ultimate solution: the increase in the slope of the CRS curve relative to rays N_3 and N_1. Consider first the labor shortage case. Let us suppose a previous situation in which N_3 had been in long-run equilibrium with a lower CRS curve at a low rate of profit. An increase in the slope of the curve would raise the rate of profit at the given capital-labor ratio. Of course, N_3 would now be in disequilibrium just as it is shown in Figure 5, and the rate of profit would tend to fall. It would only do so, however, because it had previously tended to rise; the tendency to fall signifies that there are further opportunities to increase output per man. In the working of these opposing tendencies, the disequilibrating shift of the function sets off the movement along it toward a new equilibrium at the same rate of profit as the previous *equilibrium*, but while the adjustment occurs ρ is higher. Now consider the danger of the "labor-squandering" ray N_1. Here too, if the CRS function increases sufficiently, relative to the slope of N_1, a point of tangency appears and a halt is called to the progressive deterioration of real wages. If an even greater increase occurs, then N_1 turns into N_3 and real wages rise.

What is it that causes the slope to shift? Geometrically the CRS curve may be thought to *twist* or rotate counterclockwise; or it may *stretch* upward and to the right. The economic significance of these is very different. Twisting the CRS curve to increase its slope implies a *reduction of labor's share*. This amounts to an increase in the rate of surplus value and is currently called biased growth. *Stretching* the CRS curve, neutral technological progress, increases the physical output per man without altering relative shares. This change also increases y and implies an increase in slope for each r. (See Appendix Note 5.) Both these changes raise the rate of profit.

1. Biased growth: If, in the *very long run*, an increase in the surplus population tends to weaken the bargaining position of the workers, then it may be that in the long run, the rate of surplus value, and the rate of growth of the population, are not independent of each other. In the case of the labor-squandering ray, if the workers are compelled to accept a higher rate of surplus value, the CRS curve might twist up to meet N_1. Likewise, unemployment, which results from a rate of profit less than some liquidity trap interest rate, would also raise the rate of surplus value and the rate of profit. If these long-run equilibrium rates of surplus value are still unacceptable or unbearable, then we are back to sticky factor shares as Keynes in effect suggested, and permanent labor surplus is a real ominous possibility.

2. Neutral growth: Upward stretching of the CRS curve increasing output per man would restore tangency with N_1 and escape from a low profit rate tangency with N_3. Marx did not appreciate this less painful alternative because he was be-

mused by the labor theory of value. Marx's formulation confused labor expended in national product with the product itself. Consequently, there is no way for him to satisfactorily distinguish one CRS curve from another of increased scale if factor shares are unchanged. By saying that capitalists are interested in exchange (labor) value, not use-values, Marx is led to overlook the fact that an increased flow of commodities to the capitalists *implies* increased exchange value available to them. True, they have no more "congealed labor" than before; but all that means is that their relative *share* is not altered.

The labor theory of exchange value cannot demonstrate the tendency of the rate of profit to fall. If the economy turns out more useful objects with given resources, then it matters little whether we express the process as an increase in the income to the capitalists in physical terms, or a decrease in the labor required to produce the outlay of variable and constant capital. Real wages could rise even though the rate of surplus value increased. Similarly, the labor required to reproduce a unit of constant capital also falls with technical progress. A neutral stretching of the CRS curve is equivalent to a *fall* in r. It is entirely uncertain whether the organic composition of capital tends to increase, and it actually seems to have fallen in recent years. To be sure, Marx advanced the possibility of increases in the rate of surplus value, and economies in the use of constant capital as "counteracting causes" (*Capital*, Vol. III, ch. 14) but he evidently had no idea of their potential magnitude.

5. SUMMARY AND CONCLUSIONS

From whatever perspective we view Marxism, the twofold nature of his work is evident: humanism and materialism, activism and historical inevitability, reform and revolution, truth as relative to class interest and objective science, freedom and necessity, liberty and authority, labor as a social cost and labor as the source of exchange value, "is" and "ought." Whatever the textual evidence that one of these antitheses is the "true" Marx, the fact remains that the influence of Marxism has always been stamped by this dichotomy. In the spirit of the Enlightenment, the "relative" Marx conducted a merciless dissection of conventional wisdoms from which no idea, institution, or fetish could escape as permanent or self-justifying; the "absolute" Marx strove to explain change in terms of the objective laws of motion of material forces which constitute their own justification. The contradictory aspects of Marxism have marked the social movement he has inspired; and no dialectical perfume can obliterate the spot on his doctrine. The result has been the schisms so characteristic of socialist and communist movements. Individuals, groups, and nations, attracted to the Marxian critique of capitalist property relations, have at one or another juncture had to choose between revising Marx by jettisoning his determinism, or accepting a dogma which leads to the creation of "the dictatorship of the proletariat" to replace the "dictatorship of the bourgeoisie."

The division between radical reformism and historical determinism in economics appears as the difference between the two readings of the labor theory of value we have suggested. Microeconomics is determinate in a way that macroeconomics is not, despite all the counting of propensities and equations in Keynesian models. Prices, outputs, factor combinations, and factor costs have plausible, "real," noneconomic determinants: technical possibilities, individual tastes and preferences, and initial distributions of stocks of human and material wealth. Marx's microeconomics is defective in its attempt to eliminate the subjective individual factors from the determination of value. This was more than an adherence to the conventional theory of value at the time of his writing. Marx needed a materialistic theory of value to demonstrate the exploitation of the working class and the inevitability of the collapse of capitalism. Economics had to be placed within the historical materialist science of society. Marx's analysis of exchange fails because as long as there is a range of choice of techniques and products, a satisfactory microeconomics must explain how individuals *do* shape their economic lives.

When Marx was himself confronted with the deterministic conclusions of the "dismal economists," Malthus, Ricardo, and Mill, he lashed out at their "fetishism of commodities." They mistook, he said, the social relation between men for its fantastic form, the relation between things. Man was pictured as the hapless victim of his physical environment, not its master. Contrary to the bourgeois economists, the poverty of the working class was not due to limited production possibilities which restricted the size of the wages fund; if population outran the fund of subsistence goods, it was not that there was an "absolute overpopulation," but capitalism as a social system had failed to fully develop the potentialities for increased labor productivity and regardless of the human cost had displaced workers by machinery. Workers could increase their share under capitalism by trade-union and political activity, and ultimately society could be reorganized along communist lines. Without doubt, Marx would hurl the rebuke of "fetishism" at contemporary economists who explain the distribution of income between classes by the technological possibilities of production described in various aggregate production functions. In this "relative" Marxian macroeconomics, it is the division of income between classes which restricts technology, not the reverse.

The "absolute" Marx saw everybody's fetishism of commodities but his own, and did worse than his bourgeois colleagues. Misled by the labor theory of value, he transformed Man into a material object, and made him the creature of preordained natural evolution. In economics, the fetishism took human labor as a known material entity, and caused Marx to imagine capitalism to break down due to absolute limits on the amount of value which society could produce.

Capitalism is beset with structural problems Marx identified. Classes, races, and generations may be at an impasse over differing conceptions of equity. But he did not show that capitalism will collapse of its own internal contradictions. The onus of responsibility for social change remains with those who wish to bring it about. They must nicely calculate both the good they see in their goals, and the costs entailed in the means they adopt to reach them.

APPENDIX

NOTE 1

Let $A = \begin{bmatrix} \gamma_1 & \gamma_2 \\ m_1 & m_2 \end{bmatrix}$, $F = \begin{bmatrix} F_1 \\ F_2 \end{bmatrix}$, $W = \begin{bmatrix} w_1 \\ w_2 \end{bmatrix}$,

then $AW + F = W$ and $[I - A] \, W = F$.

$$W = [I - A]^{-1} F.$$

NOTE 2

For homogeneous labor in j various industries, the Lagrangian:

$$L(V_j \lambda) = \sum_j V_i - \lambda \sum_j V_j + \sigma_j V_j.$$

Then $\dfrac{\partial L}{\partial V_j} = 1 - \lambda(1 + \sigma_j) = 0 \quad \sigma_j = \dfrac{1}{\lambda} - 1$ for all j.

Define $\qquad \zeta_j = \dfrac{v_j}{c_j + V_j}$ then $\pi_j = \dfrac{\zeta_j}{1 + \zeta_j}$

Varying ζ for each industry will result in various values for π_j.

NOTE 3

In linear programming form this question may be formulated as follows:

Minimize either $Z = \bar{\pi}'W$ or $Z' = (p\bar{\pi})'W$

$$\text{s.t.} \quad [I - A]W \geq F$$
$$W \geq 0$$

where $\bar{\pi}$ is the vector of π_i values.

NOTE 4

If we allow p_i to represent the ratio of prices of production to labor values for the i-th commodity, then reading down the columns of the matrix:

$$c_1 p_1 + v_1 p_2 + s_1 p_1 = w_1 p_1$$
$$c_2 p_1 + v_2 p_2 + s_2 p_1 = w_2 p_2.$$

Dividing through by w_i we get an expression in terms of the transpose of A:

$$A'P + \bar{\pi}P = P,$$

where $\bar{\pi} = \begin{bmatrix} \pi_1 & 0 \\ 0 & \pi_2 \end{bmatrix}$, the diagonal matrix of π_i.

Every society, then, must find a way to complete the dual linear programming problem which chooses a vector, P, such that the value of the social revenue is maximized subject to the limitation that the net rate of return not exceed $\pi_i p_i$. That is to say, the labor, w_i, is evaluated by P_i when we solve:

$$\text{Max } Z = P'F, \text{ subject to}$$
$$[I - A']P \le [\pi_i p_i]$$
$$P \ge 0.$$

A well-known property of linear programming is that the optimum values of the primal and dual are equal—total revenue and total cost are equal. Different forms of social organization, then, choose values for $\bar{\pi}$ and F, in accordance with criteria built into their institutions. Each choice implies a set of valuations, P, which are optimum *relative to that* society. An ideal socialist society would require all the p_i to be unity and would consequently choose $\pi = [I - A'][1]$ for which $Z = [1]'F$ is a maximum and surplus labor cost a minimum. Applying this set of π_i values to the primal, along with F, the Marxian optimum allocation of labor, W, may be computed. There is no reason to suppose that the π_i would be equal for all i on the socialist ethic.

The equalization of profit rates under capitalism as a ratio to stocks of assets makes the relation $s_i w_i = \pi_i$ arbitrary as well as unequal. On Marxian norms it is irrational. But the question still remains: How might a capitalist economy be described as a closed system? Given the rate of surplus value, capitalists choose the amount of constant capital and labor-power as described in part 5. By deducting the interest cost of maintaining a stock of constant capital, K, from surplus value, we get Marx's profits of enterprise, s^*. Given the market rate of interest, r, as a monitary phenomenon:

$$c^*_1 p_1 + v_1 p_2 + rK_1 p_1 + s^*_1 p_1 = w_1 p_1$$
$$c^*_2 p_1 + v_2 p_2 + rK_2 p_1 + s^*_2 p_2 = w_2 p_2$$

where s^*_i is profits of enterprise, K_i is the stock of constant capital, and c^*_i is the flow of circulating constant capital. By dividing each equation by w_i we get the following basic solution in which $k_i = K_i/w_i$:

$$[I - A'] \begin{bmatrix} p_1 \\ p_2 \end{bmatrix} = r \begin{bmatrix} k_1 & 0 \\ k_2 & 0 \end{bmatrix} \begin{bmatrix} p_1 \\ p_2 \end{bmatrix} + \pi^* \begin{bmatrix} p_1 \\ p_2 \end{bmatrix}.$$

If $\Gamma = \begin{bmatrix} k_1 & 0 \\ k_2 & 0 \end{bmatrix}$ we can write the homogeneous system:

$$[I - A' - r\Gamma] \begin{bmatrix} p_1 \\ p_2 \end{bmatrix} = \pi^* \begin{bmatrix} p_1 \\ p_2 \end{bmatrix}.$$

The ratio of profits of enterprise to labor expended, $\pi^* = s^*/w$, is an eigenvalue, since it is equalized between investments when capitalists maximize their net profits of enterprise subject to their limited *stock* of capital.

Consistent relative prices of production under capitalism can be found from the solution of the determinant equation in π^*:

$$|I - A' - r\Gamma - I\pi^*| = 0.$$

If interest is determined by "real" forces, the solution is found for $r = \pi^*$.

NOTE 5

The slope of the CRS function $dy/dr = y' = (1 - \alpha)Ar^{-\alpha}$. Slope and labor's share vary inversely: $\dfrac{\partial y'}{\partial \alpha} = - Ar^{-\alpha} - (1 - \alpha) Ar^{-\alpha} = - Ar^{-\alpha}(2 - \alpha) > 0$. Slope and A vary directly since $\dfrac{\partial y'}{\partial A} > 0$ $\dfrac{\partial y'}{\partial A} = (1 - \alpha) r^{-\alpha} > 0$.

REFERENCES

Nicholas Kaldor. *Essays in Value and Distribution.* Glencoe, Ill., The Free Press, 1960.

Eugene Kamenka. *Ethical Foundations of Marxism.* New York, Praeger, 1962.

Harvey Leibenstein. *"Allocative Efficiency vs. 'X-Efficiency',"* *American Economic Review* (June, 1966), pp. 392–415.

V. I. Lenin. *Left-Wing Communism, An Infantile Disorder,* Vol. X in *Selected Works.* New York, International Publishers, 1943.

George Lichtheim. *Marxism: A Historical and Critical Study.* New York, Praeger, 1961.

Karl Marx. *Theses on Feuerbach* in F. Engels, *Ludwig Feuerbach and The Outcome of Classical German Philosophy.* New York, International Publishers, no date.

John Stuart Mill. *A System of Logic.* Toronto, University of Toronto Press, in preparation.

Karl R. Popper. *The Open Society and its Enemies.* 4th ed. Princeton, Princeton University Press, 1963.

George J. Stigler. *"Ricardo and the 93% Labor Theory of Value,"* *American Economic Review* (June, 1958), pp. 509–23.

Benjamin Ward. *"Marxism-Horvatism: A Yugoslav Theory of Socialism,"* *American Economic Review* (June, 1967), pp. 509–23.

William A. Williams. *The Great Evasion.* New York, Quadrangle Books, 1964.

Murray Wolfson. *A Reappraisal of Marxian Economics.* New York, Columbia University Press, 1966.